IRON LUNG

Jim Goar is the author of *The Dustbowl* (Shearsman), *The Louisiana Purchase* (Rose Metal Press), and *Seoul Bus Poems* (Reality Street). His recent work can be found in *Criticism, Modern Language Studies, English, New Writing, College Literature* and *ELH*. He is an associate professor of English at Elizabeth City State University.

Also by Jim Goar

The Dustbowl   (Shearsman, 2014)

The Louisiana Purchase   (Rose Metal Press, 2011)

Seoul Bus Poems   (Reality Street, 2010)

CONTENTS

SOMETHING BLUE XXIV   11

MACHINE WITH LOVE   12

IRON LUNG 1   13

IRON LUNG 49   14

IRON LUNG 2   15

IRON LUNG 48   16

IRON LUNG 3   17

IRON LUNG 47   18

IRON LUNG 4   19

IRON LUNG 46   20

SOMETHING BLUE XVIII   21

IRON LUNG 5   22

SOMETHING BLUE XVII   23

IRON LUNG 45   24

IRON LUNG 6   26

☽   27

IRON LUNG 44   28

SOMETHING BLUE X   29

IRON LUNG 7   30

IRON LUNG 43   32

IRON LUNG 8   33

SOMETHING BLUE XVI   34

IRON LUNG 42   35

IRON LUNG 9   36

SOMETHING BLUE XXVI   37

IRON LUNG 41   38

IRON LUNG 10   39

IRON LUNG 40   40

IRON LUNG 11   41

SOMETHING BLUE XX   42

IRON LUNG 39   43

IRON LUNG 12   44

SOMETHING BLUE XXI   45

IRON LUNG 38   46

IRON LUNG 13   47

SOMETHING BLUE XV   48

IRON LUNG 37   49

IRON LUNG 14   50

SOMETHING BLUE XXII   51

IRON LUNG 36   52

IRON LUNG 15   53

SOMETHING BLUE XXIII   54

IRON LUNG 35   55

IRON LUNG 16   56

IRON LUNG 34   57

IRON LUNG 17   58

SOMETHING BLUE XXV   59

IRON LUNG 33   60

IRON LUNG 18   61

IRON LUNG 32   62

IRON LUNG 19   64

IRON LUNG 31   65

SOMETHING BLUE XXVII   66

IRON LUNG 20   67

IRON LUNG 30   68

★   69

IRON LUNG 21   70

IRON LUNG 29   71

IRON LUNG 23   73

IRON LUNG 28   74

SOMETHING BLUE XII   75

IRON LUNG 24   76

IRON LUNG 27   77

SOMETHING BLUE IX   78

IRON LUNG 25   79

IRON LUNG 26   81

ACKNOWLEDGEMENTS   83

AUTHOR'S NOTE

Iron Lung is built from the parts of three series—Iron Lung (2012-14; MS Word, 8.5" x 11", 1" margins; justified; 12 Times New Roman), Machine with Love (2015-16; Strathmore 400 Sketchbook, 8.5" x 11.5"; Sharpie .8 mm), and Something Blue (2016-18; Strathmore 400 Sketchbook, 11" x 14"; Sharpie .8 mm). The poems of each, either by number or order, are coded in the sequence of their fabrication. Two poems, traces of another series commenced and abandoned during this time, are also contained herein. *Iron Lung* was an attempt to locate and short-circuit my ideologies; I hope it causes a similar damage to you.

ISBN: 978-1-917617-11-6

The author has asserted their right to be identified as the author of this Work in accordance with the Copyright, Designs and Patents Act 1988

Cover designed by Aaron Kent

Edited by Andre Bagoo

Typeset by Aaron Kent

Broken Sleep Books Ltd
PO BOX 102
Llandysul
SA44 9BG

Iron Lung

Jim Goar

Broken Sleep Books

Red dust caught dirt that burns and spins

the gravitons ... diamond smog coal glands ... life begins

to fade from stars ... Mars what ... have ... antenna tree

A nest they say in geodesic way her belly ... airtight ... spangled free

this child of civics plied and twe beneath the ... the best are grew

in shopping malls ... supply ... supply

... strung bells to sing the song of all but you red white & blue

... seus ... a Tai ... song to ...

... I can choose ...

the ... plays me again where to start ... my

... up

... and starts the ... close

Red dust caught dirt birds burns and spins
the gravitas spills diamond smog coal plants so life begins
to fade from stars moon roof ... Mars that drives you home
smog blood Mars what lives you comb antenna tree
A nest they say in geodesic way her belly chromed airtight and spangled free
my Child of civics plied and twe by God we shape the best of you

---

Red dust caught dirt that burns and spins
before the gravitons of diamond smog coal plants a light within where a light begins airtight a light begins
to name the stars moon roof then Mars what
tick-toe tiptoe Mars bury what lives enthroned antenna tree
no feet on Mars

Combust exert
Red dust caught dirt that burns and spins
before beneath the gravitas of diamond smog coal plants night bright light begins
Tip-toe the stars moon roof then Mars by radio not right eutroned atop central tree
moon light on stars!
A nest they say in geodesic way her belly domed admitted free

beneath the gravitas
tip toe down stairs

XXV

When coal next combusts out present tense to gas in dust reposed
this bit of shell soaked sea you heard greenhouse of glass by bit exposed
slow thaw bovine carved Frankenstein tinfoil buckled nerve re-solders broken fire
birth's empty suit downs commute chalk figures purple heart bleeds out in warming air
through muted song of all went wrong encrypted traffic jams the frequency
exhaustion stalls good heavens falls deaf ears in debts grown interest free
advantage points remind annoints blue sky with glaze and ocean breeze
inject won wars et k-mart stores deadpan fort sumters anti-freeze
eyed chicken feet resigned to greet dismembered welcome script to fill
stoned into this dissolving pill invest turned about what will
to buy what tricks what each has sought inside tin man bought doomsday clock
and all the other druthers come to naught through sperm & perm the scarecrow talks
against goodnight nun-stein daylight alone believe in dark despair
no yellow road a rusted code sold engine black beyond repair

signed into this dissolving pill distressed outbreath devout what will
to buy what tricks what each has sought inside tin man stalks doomsday clock
and all the druthers come to naught through sperm and perm the scarecrow talks
against

XXV

When coal next combusts out present tense to gas in dust reposed
this bit of shell soaked sea you heard greenhouse of glass by bit exposed
slow thaw bovine carved Frankenstein tin foil buckled nerve re-solders broken fire
birth's empty suit disarms commute chalk figures purple heart bleeds out in warming air
song of all went wrong encrypted traffic jams the frequency
exhaustion stalls sky heavens calls falls deaf ears in debt grown interest free
advantage points remind annoints blue sky with glaze and ocean breeze
inject won wars et k-mart stores deadpan fort sumters anti-freeze
eyes chicken feet resigned to greet dismembered welcome script to fill
stoned into mist dissolving pill distressed outbreath devout what will
to buy what tricks what each has sought inside tin man stalks doomsday clock
and all the druthers come to naught through sperm and perm the scarecrow talks
against goodnight non-stein daylight alone beehive in dark despair
no yellow road a rusted code sold engine black beyond repair

Bird nest of hay in geodesic way a pregnant pause before decay

and chicken feet designed to greet each chopper with good day

Draft of Something Blue XXV (June 9, 2017 to July 23, 2017) page 29/34

SOMETHING BLUE XXIV

In entrance left through maze in maze through exit when
the compass points encompassed plans outbound now enters in
to knotted twine ties map design from legend pathways bend
past perfect muse refined reused webs catch what timelines send
birthright hindsight for sinister curls toward myth's foreshadowed who
then centered now the tale revolves within while prior grew
seesaw A-frame on wooded lane a cul-de-sac where children play
built middle bound by all around plot arced while page decayed
pulped minotaur Pleiades stars bent atlas under paperweight
for who goes there with hero paired a labyrinth spun from spinning gate
silkworms bookend door's orbit in a focus curved and so congrued
breath's parting crawls down lightless halls what lies behind unspooled from you
cut string to find picked up mid-line by fate combine all time had wound
half-man's set course both south and north at ouroboros source half-monster found

MACHINE WITH LOVE

/
Knowing there is
  no word
      to link
horizons as all worlds turn
so shade will face the sun
and all that between
blind to that which warns
      of place
    as it were
        designed

/
He'll contort his lake to
ship before he's worth
his salt that means
he's come undone
      in inland seas
    to call a wave a wave
beyond its depth   behind
       the boy-
    ant   wood
and blades of dew refrain

/
  This foothold
assembled as landlocked
  by green wood and my arbor
      a machine with love

Man is framed by his own projections. The material world functions apart from quixotic influence. There is nothing in film but an absence of light. The goods we've created have created our heads. I'm prostate before igloos of diminishing return. Ask not what your country has deposited in you. Genealogies redistribute our dearly departed. My interest compounds behind matrimonial borders. Abrogate a box of dark matter when the curtains ascend. Redundancies keep all isotopes home.

My authentic response's unbroken agreement builds spellbinding nonsense another resplendent vehicle for ethical transmission. Each figurehead's disembodied appearance showers nondescript safewords from jaw locking orthodoxy's cannibalizing defacements. Behind whose highfalutin guardrail do alphabetical fictions silently repair in cold mouths shivering with common parlance? Her shapeshifting monologue's circumscribed receiver forever preserves hermeneutically infused memories of amber enthroned intrusions. Our blood-soaked progeny's lyrical encasements riffle through unrequited stethoscopes embraced beneath a flesh eating monument's continental divide.

Generic cosmopolitans appropriate indigenous migrations. States cede historical revisions to their corporate sponsors. The automobile commercials are post-agrarian here as well. Wherever immaculate consumption romanticizes a hemorrhaging wilderness, the Tin Man's corrosive narrative is coated by Dorothy's emblematic influence. Televised famines ache for the days of antiquated resistance. Which hemisphere did we litigate first? I sleep best under auctioned climes. Ours being the language savages have always spoken. A shinning tractor is necessary for your pharmaceutical joy.

Childhood's linear abandonment brokers backslapping estates contained within an antibacterial suburbia's formfitting vocation. My incest bearing marriage embraces these self-styled genomes confessing homogenized faith in heterosexual emporiums lugubriously aligned. Whose bouncing progeny doesn't push through nameless glands imbibing swings we sat astride some milquetoast newborn's financial reprise? Our holiday season's gendered investments dutifully namedropped Mohammedan choirs from choreographed ringtones' overheard elision. Each irreversible father's intergenerational utterance recapitulates the myths man's shed for family goes without saying.

Anyone who declares their interdependence is caught in a net. The break-down of collaborative systems has legitimized the increased jurisdiction of citizen police. We didn't ask any questions before she was absorbed by an expanding grammatical corruption. Each sentient being conforms to un-verifiable hands. Manifest destiny was intimately tied to the cerebral harvest of sperm whale ardor. Numbers tell the story insofar as dogma is listening. At issue is our inability to endear ourselves to a permanently united state.

Chivalry's twilit spring bearer stands before wedding showers to witness equinoxial regeneration in her unifying way. This hypersexualized aura of coexistence manhandles golden years vented through soul searching fertility's reproductive foreskin. What bearded woman's two-faced ovum uproots maximum security's chain-link defenses so man remains benighted inside panorama's unmitigated absorption? Each reigning benediction's noble biopic shepherds sovereign usurpers toward storefront propriety's excommunicated confection. His wellborn cavalry's death-defying incantations muster downhill momentum enthroned about an overdubbed archrival's purest form.

Security is forged in alliance with conservative notions. Middleclass stability prospers behind iron-curtains. It is an untenable language which expands where the mute lay pixilated. Your engine injects an expulsion of others crafted from the ruins of my individualized world. I am an exploiter in this means of salvation. Morality backs each citizen into a prefabricated fortress. We've come to babble by the lucrative practice of witchcraft. Death is a contingency for whose reappearance? Segregation negates the freedom of all.

Our inside voice's eye-catching production subtracts headwinds through strumpets of intellectual causation's diaphanous relief. This brainwashed station's unfolding extension encases masculine preservation's delineated encampment in learned society's ontological catcall. What about-faced hourglass wraps the watchword's punctual homogeneity around his trusted amnesia's two-timing brow? Wholehearted purity's tell-tale death march silently proceeds from concrete attempts at an asymmetrical lovechild's well-rounded surcease. My sure-sighted normality's bilocated animus violently delivers makeshift remainders for every reigning fallacy's most bearable continuation.

SOMETHING BLUE XVIII

Inherited can't without reciting what brokered knot should end lines meet

to man they say what man will be your TV eyes on every street

sidewalk his view from me through you between us two to bind with practiced grace

now he we too combined as puzzles grew coupled to grid the common place

all hopes and dreams on drive through screens without receipt return to you

new broken ties a white lie's prize from heirloom be a gift of something blue

and so do minds unwind blurred highway signs the car seat mapped by wedded words

this given lot to like or not for passing thought evicts no one who left remembers what they heard

to stich in time to sew betwixt betwine to face begotten face

as one and you as others do to them we kiss our dear returned to be replaced

so by and by in seamstress eye worn oversight patched inmate found interned anew

this back and forth forced out resourced we lace two feet to fit in compound shoe

instep half-step a foot too far astride crossroads dismember what we say and do

so with that in tow you're free to stay or go inside two-face foreseen the other through

Every boy now lives in a bubble. Internal optics fuel transpersonal divides.
We must first isolate acts ingested through observation. The guillotine is
memory's physical means of transportation. Watch how demarcations shape
our TV Dinners. Inherited penitentiaries metabolize the ontological proof from
which societies ascend. These unverifiable collusions don't require a footnote
of departure. What in depth necessitates continued disappearance? Famines ex-
hume byproducts of antisocial institutions coalesced around ephemeral order.

SOMETHING BLUE XVII

Past is spinning past so only what alas was present there
two stories revolving clockwise and counter round on tether constricting timeline shared
the we we build ourself today while looking backward lifetime hence
and mark each moment where to start a path to present recompense
to breathe the past the past has sown in iron lung red blood and bone
the unrelenting bust of ground through first man spade in garden grown
this stained glass heart a greenhouse built of parts unknown
whose shadows dance projected onto curtain falls within ancestral home
to waltz a stanza glowing bright through doors once left now open right
the headway into black and white in house to end with dying light
we make this day unreel as yesterday was once believed
upon a time when day before in mobile home a static home conceived
of earthen halls displayed on mirrored walls a still life made of landlocked man
to frame in light bisect by sight by anchor root this statue stands

My quarry's concrete halls arterially redistribute effigies across the worldwide conglomerate's ever molting consumption space. Each agoraphobic production's auto-possessing delay infuses deadlocked afterthought with drive through windows opened on mystical byways. What discount menu mustered invisible hemispheres forever concealing our subaltern shell's proprietary sky? A fictive memory's naturalized diabetic awaits stoplights cycling her grandfather's blue-collar attempts at multistate transit. This overdetermined immigrant's atmospheric encasement siphons anonymous foodstuff praised for selflessly delivering recognizable brands of nostalgic emission.

/

Our composite sky repeats

its thought called blue becomes

my heart as though my heart

blooms moon for you

and only you   the birds have

flowered into their unborn land

beneath the compound words

this sunburnt dirt embodies

/

To unite as one

with your hands

in the welding sound

as we mermaid beneath

begetting moons

like a still life led

to happy flotsam

after each cohabitated

rabbit ear is sewn

/

The old charts ring true to

themselves and build for you

at once inhabited already

converted a woman through

etchings of birth embossed

each outstretched hand

to mold the earth and sunder

a flattened land they saw with care

Nationalism is a self perpetuating abstraction. Memorial Day resonates with songs of surplus value. This theatrical rebellion furthers manifold relations masking oppression. An utterance isn't bound by etymology but by the laws that cover it. Freedom's idealistic dogma forever mystifies those tied to its moorings. We are the product of cosmic husbandry. Patriotism stills my beating heart absent carbon's ecological cohabitations. Why must Taps crescendo into superstition? Spectacle is woven through eons of static.

☽

Nothing matters this moon on white page

      the pastoral allusion
      measured by willows
      all branded in speak

   hidden behind eyelids
      as cowboys behind cows

more come home to roost
   through concepts removed

            an eardrum compares to night's face

          each diphthong
       makes way for its spoon

Waking vision's seraphic hindsight acquires seams intact from blood let soil moved sufficiently by corollaries delivering fictive notes. Our compact mirror's timeless calendar instantaneously configures its polemic in space giving my countenance the certain appearance of second nature. Whose overlooked caliphate's underground moment designs thy true self's everlasting surface? This restorative abatement's serrated ampersand embraces stigmatized communities throughout an auto-replicating contour's re-founding incision. Historical anesthesia's gaseous conjunction selectively imposes spellbinding constraints on every animated conspirator's postoperative body.

SOMETHING BLUE X

Man's sent through post-production as history's written in
forgotten language lost as Sappho's poems begin
buttressed by virgin forest with manifest destiny on one side
worlds that would be sight unseen now causally divide
but what was fore annexed by next abyss forever hides
this initial concept from it itself itself it says surmised
supporting beams fell all collapsing schemes and it alone survived
to brake the bone from dirt to dig a neoliberal beehive
whose deeds are sold on grounds from which society anew will rise
from knee to shinning knee to stand before the workaday decay
with much ado and nothing new erections fade away
but away requires a there which binds imagined homes deprived
so when I doff my cap to sing this past this way arrived

Humans grasp at metaphysical walls and their calcifications. Everything we hold dear is premised by deepening opacity. How to envision paraphrases budding assarts from the trees? Gravity receives feedback from within its falling influence. There is no peripatetic continuation on continental shelves or preserves. Evolution divides at the axiom of extinction. What is unborn is no less hungry for tropical-flesh-itself. Topography encircles man's esoteric liminalities. An unfolding universe packs a lunch for all that moves away.

/

I've returned unsure
for thoughts are thinking
for words are roots
all practiced to face the ears
insert syntax before a mask
they stand to sing
a song they'll never hear

/

Nature is a symbol
to fence pastoral goods
we build a sky
while neighbors watch
personified within the
light of man reposed
to shade on bended knee

/

Dusk becomes to say
an April harp contains
these rounding words
grown sky and red
with bees alike
on flowers landing

A recorded history's autonomous eyewitness steadily consumes unimpeachable diktats survived by legislative roots of subsidized perdition. These duly noted trespasses link genomes towering over pupils repatriated at matriculation's orderly accounting. During what law abiding assent did lady justice cede housebroken men their inherited cells stacked with papers demarking the dearly departed? Our divisible education's colorblind offspring pass through racial birthrights ascribing physics whatever outrage cements my earmarked condition. Each collectively erected tenement layers transgressions on socialized bodies covered in branded submission's impenetrable shawl.

Primitive nomenclatures construct silos above our fields of endeavor. An urbanized multitude remains entranced by indoctrination's monotheistic spell. We expire in the shade of crystallized taxonomies blossoming from superstitious roots. Etymological motivations are catalogued to strengthen indivisible restraints. How can I isolate this pretext when every invoice cultivates prefabricated contrition? A standing army's unbending sword hoards antiquated metaphor from the subway's repetitive orbit. Medieval catacombs eclipse the grammar of cities where pastoral sidewalks end.

SOMETHING BLUE XVI

The boughs of headwind past unto a present perfect break
in ears to find against the tide the breath the sea will take
by sky by sea by mast in dying light lulled from sun and into night
this internal turning gaze in breaking day illuminates despite
the forces of a rising moon invented and eclipsed
disseminated across dark skies for in half-life the day by day has missed
an eye inspecting out of sight and mind unseen inside will hold
this opposite below the mended double vision insight the night twofold
guiding movements from where we say not there but deeper in a long-lost face
to come undone from sleep another sleeper's notes misplaced
for it is me to be before the wooden dreams the chosen words of me do make
from catbird seat my eye to lighthouse lie buoyant on the starboard wake
and so inclined on port medieval lands the mermaid of my better half
hobbled both in and out the nautical keep from cradle fell this well-worn path

Orchestrated happenstance illuminates long-term caregivers of geometric perspective at state in a still life's figurative montage. His handmaiden's brushstroke somatically lingered on candlelit phantoms whilst carpet baggers parlayed their ceasefire's creative omission. What enlightenment remains when contemporary eyes behold our disembodied century's semantic plunder uncoiling institutionalized esthetic's exclusionary canvas? These chemically formulated quarantines harken back to transatlantic cables moored by cordon sanitaire's epidemic delight. Each fading martyr's piercing bosom incites the hungry cups amassed behind her velvet curtain closed for civic repair.

Terraformation's palimpsest reproduces through countless states of variation. Urban majesty is a modern pastoral written atop environmental symbiosis. These vertical borders conjugate terracotta with cartographic charts. Our North American cityscapes bleed from countless pockets of evangelistic amalgamation. What remains preserved in primordial fragments besides opaque attachments? Gentrified catacombs repatriate legislative channels by subverting postmodern's polyphonic expositions. A suburb's reconstructive discourse paves over revisionist sinkholes with manufactured consent.

SOMETHING BLUE XXVI

What madness roused to white hot tears slouched toward our public land
defeat informs by goosestep swarm into a park where law disbands
hate oxidized round mounted lies pressure applied moves what was still
forged rivets rust in god we trust old statutes strode through Charlottesville
Flint's lead downstream dog whistle meme sound views reflect their echoed worth
where mermaids laid manned barricade lost cause conveyed flame's hallowed earth
from broken notes burnt Nero learned by hanging chad election turned
to stand your ground till all fall down confetti bloat war dead have earned
red stripes above great wall foresworn on antebellum map a new day born
of flagged decrees linked twitter feeds embraced relief as Irma stormed
across the beached seashell eared men bore tiki torches come again
to tilt at shale's wind powered spin a time capsule ajar within
lives UDC's gaslights erect to consecrate what then as now we should regret
up to our knees our landfill bleeds bequeathed the peace of tourniquets

Occupation's opposing thumbs kneed confectionary reality with children assuming duplication's plainspoken view. This oft broken word's false equivalency collates xeroxed referents appearing unchanged beneath thy loving hand's sweetest duress. What unwritten doctrine silently mobilizes accountable reflections agreeing to stand before their blood stained hour's untimely retreat? Each double-checked box remains buried in nostalgia's outdated lockers for post-productive memory's collaborative affect. Our time-honored allusions reciprocate the skeleton keystroke's soft-spoken introduction of colloquial continuity drawn through impacted vocabulary's colliding stop signs.

The iron lung echoes with predetermined pangs of evolutionary zeal. Man's compulsory respiration casts societal firmaments on propagation's immutable bouquet. Each illegitimate emancipation in turn attempts to father Theogony's digestive arrangement. Stepchildren spring from layers of compartmentalized abyss and I am yours. Exaltation's recessive creeds gather beneath our jungle gym proper. Whose remains metastasize an applecart's hereditary skinnings? Chloroplasts transcend synaptic admonishment by fulfilling the dead with air.

My present anxiety lays unambiguous hips on succulent display unseating fabricated expatriates with procreation's nostalgic mail-orders. Connective virtues' embracing renunciations turnabout autoerotic interventions reminiscing through truelove's destabilizing conviction. Beneath whose idiomatic cantilever does sexuality's umbilical high wire wantonize official forms of nonsensical come hithers? This benevolently obstructed sightline supersedes self-criticism's socio-economic implications by naturalizing each genuflecting acolyte's covetous reflection. Our ergonomically selective manikins sell life-threatening remission from circumscription's engendered camcorder.

Humanity ties remnants of old bouquets to new and modified forms. Our reproductive traditions consecrate inorganic borders by legislating nuclear cohabitation's misanthropic shell. Mummified offspring yield germinative affections to technology's necromantic arbiters. What unverifiable network mitigates my primordial foundations? Cybercryptic versification captures extramarital transmissions in intricate webs of filial polarization. A privatized menagerie fathers absent relations with the crown's democratic inhabitants.

SOMETHING BLUE XX

Shadows before foreshadows of doubt forewarned
dismissed still sunlight spotlit white walls wildfires adorned
a window hung in liminal climes outshined by better time's pastoral vision
year by year decreased who saw inside the frame bespoke with secondhand elision
this lens craft mends our present tense we light the gaze one stormy night
till all burn bright when lights go dim so eyes adjust today's foresight
to be what previews me from me to be what was to come has now foretold
from in my storied background life the lifelike waits in times of old
where white washed land tilled soil to sand to fill the rascally rabbit hole
this hourglass of falling hearts to fall inside one side half full
of old film stock we make still life at blackened hearths in light of doubt
the gulf between the worlds revolves the hence from whence now files out
to back away on horseshoes tossed this splitting ends in disbelief
for shadows know which way to go in darkness grasped for stark relief

Nostalgia's catalytic conversions implement homogeneity by redressing footnotes predisposed to an individual's belated edification. Our sanitized ink spots celebrate cordial words on congested streets where architectural exonerations mandate tribunal adherence from whence all harmonized incantations forever collide. What nerve-racked lampshade illuminates cartographic destinations now that skylined curtains have overcast horizon's prefabricated dawn? This backyard raven's landlocked revelry orates discord from inside childhood strongholds of snow globe delight. Each steadfast homeowner commutes mimetic aggregation misquoting security's exordial swansong.

Neural contaminants spread beyond their ports of origin. Democracy's telescopic sideshow hobbles men with exotic infatuations. Each encore's ovation is soldered by Nagasaki's laughing stock. These post-colonial shibboleths demonstrate a latent conquistador's seditious intentions. Social undercurrents coagulate bloodlines ionically deployed across the iron-clad-sea. Why should disembodied combatants instigate spontaneous acts of mutual combustion? Trenched feet bridge the void between a maiden and her maker. Archaic frameworks come to nothing in the end.

SOMETHING BLUE XXI

When this divided house collides again and comes unbound
and sand reforms our social norms in ocean sound
the hills both wet and warm with mother's milk
will loose the fire tooth in flags and of their ilk
flooding from the coast and what is burning from within
to make the new the same inclined to turn the other's cheek again
these gains by smoke and mirror repeated and appraised
for those who've saved the most have others wrought what they have made
and those made pliant goods for gods are gathered need
each self-preservation undercut by reservations raised around endangered creed
so now this skin tight ghetto's fashion forms a lesser kin
whose covered heart is pledged in warning signs embody each American
devoted confusion reigns when everyman is swept into a middle ground
and man is fused by what he hewed and not the other way around

Auto-correcting search engines recalibrate hunger's empirical manifestations through which we maintain only penury. Nanotechnology's limitless deflections solder one-way-tickets to retailers imparting mimetic liberations gestated inside our disposable bodies. What soliloquized moment sustains expired provisions for some supermarket branding scarcity amongst her wholehearted production's shinning isles? Each bargain hunter becomes the voice of universal communication picked over by harmless words turned unto fingers. Monetized society's self-serving destitution barcodes globally occurring concessions whose financial seeds restore a crowded checkout line.

Children fill the open mouths of bipeds loaded for transfer. Progeny's multiple iterations systematically recalibrate each surrogate's asymptomatic reflection. This evolutionary redistribution of hegemonic discourse is muted by an info-mercial's tribal muster. Cherubic incantations conceal the reigning oligarchy's congenital decline. What pasteurized language induces introspection beneath its baited breath? Idiomatic staples ensure my tongue is tied to an embalmed cadaver's defining order. Recursive traditions descend upon eternal divides.

SOMETHING BLUE XV

Man folds man inwards in next of kin
portrayed what scissors made united by outlining him
mouth to mouth in breeding binds each nesting in maternal twin
but turned about and inside out an outside voice revolving in
to cut in line of sight through eyelets laced to face the face of everyday
where only some of what went in in only parts of speech from some have stayed
this common fraction unable to insooth yet doth convey
past to present tense the waking of a dream delayed
to hold a promissory note the middle aged accordion
says at least we talk this way both in and out of what has been
for man repeats their half and whole again from him is pulled away
attached to one half more creating paper men in hand to hand our hands display

Habitual machines design picturesque rows of identical milestones forever preserving a weekday migration's harmonious interior. This midcentury spectacle retains electronically updated heroes converted at toll-booths to change before my carpool's emergency broadcast reply. Under whose natural order does the astronaut's repeated leaps and bounds silently traverse inoperable space on her branching comet's unfolding entrails? Our televised memories divine foregone conclusions reflecting an auto-tuned biosphere's unforeseeable private-eyes. Each inherited function's given name conceals its storebought lineage with indispensable arms entreating sugarcoats surround us.

American ideology projects safe harbor on the back of a multitude hidden away.
Identical aerials redistribute likeminded earrings and uprisings from the television
set for exotic production. This epoch's industrial sprawl is nothing but a well worn
embrace of a tutor's reflected border. Our inland empire shutters the exit through
which illuminated sunstones commute beyond Cartesian mantra. I am willingly
imprisoned in a bosom of exogenic ornamentations. Why salvage trinkets left
on antiquity's excavated wake? Every lighthouse precipitates its theater of rust.

SOMETHING BLUE XXII

Detached words slip from lips' accrued semantic hold
beneath behest below bedrest the riddled ground states life twofold
this great divide bequeaths implied namesake denied in aether roam
between the who of me and such was you midway waylaid one halfway home
displaced inside this seeking hide sewn button fly Rosetta Stone
missteps ring forth round tethered source past footnotes sunk unseen rhizome
for there resides comingled lives repair upstairs stained glass enshrines the story told
by neural thief to end night's brief rotation now your focal point controlled
with eye's own mind thy muddled sign revision mimes the clearest sight is dulled
so what sees you in puddle viewed enfant though art at last a future mold
conjunct assign dead words to mine with stammer lock a jailor by the seed to stow
sown salt and mirth on mother earth from syntax anchored subtexts grow
a fatherland where sea meets sand to feed the host that's never full
so more some lay in plotted graves each headstone claimed by flag and soul

Evolution's metastatic reverberations facilitate aleatory giddiness on whatever short-circuit my simulacrum requires. Deconstructed torrents unfold imagery's orbital system without impeding kingdoms precipitated by each pixelated past. What reflected proclamation cursorily wrests these human remains from thy unassailable lip overburdened forthwith refined neutrality's digitalized production? All propriety lines insolate blood relations through neck-in-neck distribution walled up inside forged meritocracy's teaming divide. Networked sensuality's prophylactic investment clandestinely extols camaraderie's restitution crouched beneath a mistletoe's architectural reply.

Enlightenment's seductive narrative conceals a vanguard's encroaching credenda. Tradition's mnemonic renunciations remain intertwined with the circuitous network our catechisms purportedly transcend. Each penitential text fastens authorial discourse to unblinking eyes. These polyphonic appeals filter autonomous speakers through various ceremonial functions of historical construction. How many indifferent lenses coax muted abstraction from an ideologue's alienated tongue? I am a vocabulary moored to its codex of canonical engagements. Myopia blossoms in sanctified sums.

SOMETHING BLUE XXIII

When double bind's contested mine encircles back to back before
and what repaired with thine ensnared we reach resolve in knotted core
then whiled away my dear delay a pirouette turned earth out of a point retold
this Christmas wreath whole heart belief stands in for you as you unfold
across the tongue tied dawning space details expand what's never full
of dying day by birth waylay dusk's question cast on borrowed foal
wherein withdrew new shadow grew from ear out to the mount explained
remarked by sound rode upside down who can recall who can't remain
our love bore you in head of who now please construe what needs to be
raised hands alight jailbirds take flight these stories hold beyond the sight you see
where mind alone itself unknown to self who calls from wishing well within
by endless grace still watered face upturned for who as you descend to look again
while down you go past ice that rose through falling snow
back to a wellborn nesting place to wait what awl the next will know

Pregnancy's captivating narrative delivers transformative ideologies to posterity's internalized audience announcing dialectics have been dismantled. Each populated reflection communicates an effervescent armistice by exceeding man's predicated movement we retrospectively occasion. What unifying criterion remains unacknowledged so certain terrors run operational and returned they disappear? My subsequent question exhumes antiquity's limitless internment recast beneath the groundbreaking vanguard's regenerative embrace. These eroticized subtropics posthumously domesticate a virgin forest's glass coffin with archival photos conceiving our crowning truelove.

Cognition matriculates through quarantined grids under continuous gaze. To counterbalance internal optics a preening student mirrors the phenomenal world's heterotopic liberations. Who is able to explain their privileged persona suspended between these interdisciplinary mechanisms of power? Education's superimposed backdrops reproduce asymptomatic hierarchies which normalize asymmetrical relations. I am conclusively annihilated by uncanny protagonists fermenting domesticated objects of disassociation. Analysis trains prescriptive beacons on the darkness emanating from an absent body.

Centralized missives christen the separatist function's elliptical attestation with tongue-in-cheek odysseys integrated as supplements constructed. This multilingual operation's circuitous revision designates a rubbernecked spectrum through which seaworthy matrons shouldn't otherwise elide. What untold man-of-war must reunite metastasized reservoirs on misbegotten statements before all wonders forsaken for speech can finally be undone? No terminology disrobes its letters whose absence conducts each lovelorn consumer's regenerative purpose. My heartfelt collusions further sentimentality's obscurant lineage so that bon voyage will hardly find surcease despite another.

Dialogue's parapenal architecture shapes the discursive practice by which an individual meets his maker. Hyperbolized purifications rummage aristocratic growth from endless attics of introverted attacks. Why should each genome's vicarious inquisitions continually establish archival rules for my embedded attestations? Our authority to perform a normative function has permanently withdrawn behind anonymous artifices of in vitro fetishizations. Far from its theatrical unveiling, this text transmits the disease I was composed to redact.

SOMETHING BLUE XXV

As oil in dust refines our present tense we lie in past's repose
this bit of shell soaked sea you heard greenhouse of glass by bit exposed
slow thaw bovine carved Frankenstein tinfoil touched nerve to solder broken fare
sheep's empty suit disarms dispute chalk figures' purple hearts bleed out in warming air
mild winter song of all went wrong encrypted traffic jams the frequency
a honeyed creed's metastatic seeds commute in sweet hyperbole
advantage points remind anoints blue sky with glaze and ocean breeze
ingest what fors at surplus stores deadpan Fort Sumter's antifreeze
bomb shelter feast mushroomed defeat byproduct of drunk hemlock paid
war chest of hay in geodesic way a pregnant pause before decay
confined what ticks what each has sought inside Tin Man a doomsday clock
when all the druthers come to naught born out of turn the scarecrows flock
unto midnight nonstick daylight high noon arrives in dark despair
no yellow road a rusted code the engine block beyond repair

Steadfast terminology contextualizes an implicit straw man's predetermined relation betwixt two static spheres hermetically sealing disunion. This uniformed vocabulary partitions chain reaction by curating furtive heterodoxies reorienting inside its occidentally motionless resolution. Under whose unbending guidance do surrogates emit repeated movements arching beyond the ironclad keystone's bicentennial decline? Our antisocial footnotes become another systemic entanglement invariably tied to fictionalized umbrellas decried in moderate debate. Each pineal constellation's overhead compartment infuses illiterate classes with mystical renditions of dawn's fading light.

Procreation's unnamed eventualities fabricate ciphers of micro-disturbances earmarked to ensure their carefully maintained permission. Interpersonal armistices entomb irruptive truth beneath a sword's performative utterance. What parliamentary crusade does not camouflage paramilitary entitlements in tomfoolery's vainglorious disrepair? Feudalism's agricultural values derive our disembodied inhabitants from threnody's benevolent root. This honorable conflagration showers enviable virtues on the consecrated furrow of pejorative order. Modernity's refurbished vernacular paints decaying aristocracies with popular despair.

Itinerant missionaries circumnavigate cathartic orthodoxies unbeknownst to the decommissioned conductor's iconoclastic throng. Our most somnolent operatives flicker offstage before collective happenstance admits a homespun thespian's aborted revival. By whence does this disarticulated gramophone's riveting omission emblazon suffragettes on linoleum appropriations of husbandry defied? An ethnographer's multinational mispronunciations coax ever-present disarmament from future generations evolving inside their hallmarked retreat. Each standing archive's transmutable coercion purports exuberance for conflicting etymology only demarcation can honorably excise.

/

To sit a bird
for whitened shit
upon the page
from left to right
a model bird
behind this dead man's curve
displayed its movement
cursive splayed
toward I to think
what next reposed
a bit downstream
from marble cutters' grace

/

When after the eye concedes
and every border finds its rest
a moon pronounces you
for stars imagined sundrenched fences
behold a concept naming
this downturned face repeats itself
as earth surrounds our chain link toes

/

Because the dirt
Beneath my nails
Dreams in leaves

Hermetic nativities vilify metaphysical trespasses bivouacked amongst gentrification's canonical developments. Why condemn unto dreams these endlessly milling excisements or reactivated territory awakened therein? The necromantically moderated have hashtagged their yearnings with secrets consumed by enigma's cathartic advances. Every foundational enactment is carefully enunciated through rebellion's emancipated vocabulary of prescriptive addiction. My anatomic designs reduce to artifice within this symposium's disquieting arena. A somnolent madness forever marks our numerous infractions against the reflexive void.

Incarceration's laborious bounties remain unascertainable without the postcolonial headhunter's whitewashed defacement. Every concurrent circuit's anonymous participants obfuscate welfare queens amassed behind some wineglass lit in agricultural afterglow. How could discursivity sung from mounted facsimiles reposition terminology befitting classical education recalled around a heartland's formfitting net? These impersonal situations have taken for granted an uncircumcised lineage cast heavenly against vicarious anxiety's woebegone renown. Our ethical penitentiary's inner annexations authenticate uroboric consumers before their closing cistern's mimetic respite.

Glazed hurricane by lighthouse twist tin soldiers cast to magnet sun
rotating pleats dress slacks storm gray impact the drains so streets will run
gene pools ring true tide's Elmer's Glue harbored conquests rain praise upon
torn photo glare glossed midnight hair cleft lip to slip through cracks of dawn
dark face dark face so full of grace come out come out of hiding place
warm isle beheld current's embrace French kiss embossed salt's aftertaste
momentum broke canned worms mint waves of sugar grown on shallow graves
the cost encased in human trade love lost to sail doldrums' malaise
across the landlocked gulf's volcanic flume sunk wishing well lure's spark illumes
what filters blood's subtropic plume light caught whale breath treed plankton bloom
man's handmade chains link seasick sound fed daily toil as cargo bound
to gather close those dear around flashed mirrored face in rubble found
the cracks the cracks break mothers' backs snapshot consumed glass living room
in image raised on serving spoon customs import what floods exhume

Accordial confessions convert a conquistador's expanding curiosity into restive memories of imperial transmission. This synthesizing activity is invaded by answers my oldest illusions artfully homage for latent discovery. We are bifurcated by two thousand years of archival cacophony unzipping the ocean blue. Why should our indentured nostalgia inherit serpentine pleasures cobbled beneath introspection's rectangular table? Exoticisms are finalized in a sextant's empirical imagination. Consumptive ecologies radiate majestic continents awaiting redemptive sails.

Blubbered neologisms pantomime selfhood framed by cranial spheres ultrasonically resounding authentic dawning's redundant production. This loquacious lantern's unspeakable sextant astrally inflates individuals beyond the decomposing animal which periodically replicates its aboriginal forbearer. On whose cultivated palate should gerunds sway over colloquial minnows entertaining metaphysical encasements triumphant at death? Each shipwrecked cacophony has sewn disunion through a voice box waxed for autonomy's automated promise. Our sinking vessel's spermaceti organ herds luminous subtropics to codified boneyards beneath the fisherman's unrelenting cap.

★

Let us not begin with plums
　　　　in driftwood glass. These
　　　　　upturned
　　pits for stars like all
　　　unravel. Come rain against
　but lettered stems spit time before.

Let us not begin with plans.

Let us not in tree top naves
　erect dry bones
　to harvest seed. Let headwinds'
crest prolong the night. Let winnowed
words burn salt from withstood sea.

Technicolor panoramas admit westernized imaginations through Oriental ports. These automated visions fashion sanitized adolescents from didactic embodiments of institutionalized opticians. What do indigenous trademarks signify now that our embargo's illuminated enjambments posit fictions staged for an exclusive audience's transnational manifestation? Each billboard's eternity levies sensual conscriptions on productive beds in ephemeral locution. My choreographed appropriations oscillate between the despotic and quixotic with only humanity's assumptive role to play.

America's lily-white reservations beget unsustainable lineages protected from deep inside our erected horizon's array of invisible penumbra. These repetitive revitalizations phonetically instill nostalgic testimony atop said urban planner's vivisected confection. By whose elevated vantage should my genealogical allotment's plotted twine redistrict cosmetic kettling's communicative visage? The unnerving market's metastasized aesthetics laud sedentary writs with gastric lockets shorn from a blueblood's omnipresent pauper. Each clandestine union spreads over sanitation's subterranean apparatus in all manner akin to an abscess absent fracking's aquatic displacement.

/

At the time of writing
destruction is within
a they unfolding
if each is absent we
thread and through
each excrement of sky
is how the unborn grows
a life unlike itself

/

All words made in words
their prior is nothing but
without nothing as all things
becoming as though waiting
before a word has spoken
as I have said there
here was there exhaling

/

If that was my
time in shade
to gin inside
a friend whose feast recedes
the gift of any bird
who lays in distance grows
a pot about its future feed

Pejorative enticements germinate mimetic constellations demarking the limits of liminal cognition. Industry's overdetermined imaginations manufacture metaphysical inertia hostile to transformation's evolutionary energetics. Why must surplus commute between weekday rituals on seasons harvesting indentured outcroppings? My familiar restraints foster emancipatory assumptions unable to articulate our festively coercive ephemera. This revolutionary era descends upon its subjects cast in bonded circulation. Metamorphic erosions fall for lines divined behind an electorally ennobled screen.

Fabled artifacts broadcast alchemic permissions masquerading as deities retreating throughout our programed modality. Each dogma's cloistered assets opt for Saturn's iron ring to elevate a piston like so many miniature pontiffs hung above an almshouse knell. At what ungodly hour did Galahad's impersonal digressions ascend beyond his sinewy abandon's anamorphic forgiveness? This spectacle's creolized carnival corresponds without illuminated antlers amassing before the inexhaustible archetype's reproductive machinery. My mythological antonym restrains its most resplendent unfolding in living rooms unwrapping a rebooted festivity's unvanquished award.

SOMETHING BLUE XII

When the commons clearcut is sold as cost
        unto itself a custom claims
to be tongue tied in family tree
        with self but not itself the same
not framed in newborn light and means
        itself now smelt in debted shade
to pay the pound of flesh the axe induced
        the self another self has made
amongst the birds and bees
        her spreading knees a will of love surnamed
dividing him in equal parts
        for divided men in hock remain
this less than none now all undone
        without a sound waylaid
its beating heart for that too parts
        as nothing itself can stay
on borrowed time from last in line
        and what the never mind has lent
this auctioned ground pulled all around
        for life from life is rent

Industrialists recall utopia's exceptional isolation through an interdependent mythology obfuscating immutable contacts. This naturalized innovation offshores responsibly for the recidivist foundations supporting paucity's lucrative practice. Why do consumers procreate mimetic entrepreneurs scolded in capital's sepulcher embrace? Our society's instant messages furnish denizens generously endowed with punctual ovulations facing time-honored constraints. Modern technology enlivens the means by which each profit is partitioned. Financial ruins run counter to my status inlaid on broadband's proclivity.

Bombsites ring from closed captions inwardly mouthing all syncopated community in an intervention's unfamiliar voice. Every hallowed a cappella is cordially drawn to entrenched photography's muted apparatus our stillborn waged beneath ancestral eyes. Whose tongues untie my fortune's regenerative victim with shaking hands commissioned for conflagration's perpetual commiseration? Clockwise bridges fall on sepia tables' ascending echoes of those who heft odd books onto a café's barricaded stage. This metronome's time lapsed mechanism systematically constructs incendiary devices unsaying counterrevolution's irretrievable past.

SOMETHING BLUE IX

What is lost in knowledge won
but that what which was before
before set out is now undone
for beforehand's what which once at once implored
is disavowed before the war of words our overseers moor
to beget what has begotten of what is once again set free
but free from what is what a what can never truly be
this troubled time as now a what went past a past restored
to walk to count of ten but turn and turn again and there are more
and more behind before the disembodied turning thing
which embraces mirrored fingers in a double helix wedding ring
that circles back to back on what itself itself believes
for what behind again moves forward into what enclosed foresees

This inborn itinerary is coordinated by collated fragments that compartmentalize what contorts to become a contiguous individual. Incomplete eviscerations compound incoherent connections between two molten conjunctions and my subsequent crime. Who is language but an automated republic engendered with insufficient resistance for undermining the concealing process which propagates itself? Generations scrawl across hydroelectric towers their familiar misnomers tying salt waters to her algebraic moon. Our ideal impediment communicates man's expansive vision freed from emancipated metaphor entrusted beneath encrusted leaves of Sunday's papier-mâché.

/

Take care how you
inscribed with roommate sought
how I in stanza speak
my heart upon itself
till what remains to see
are works of elegant words
reviewed in ghostly sequence
by this past reader in your stead

/

Our world recited
and in this field recast
green leaves as gold
on knees of eloquent hay
manufacturing commonplace discovery
that little moisture appears in print
and ink in such dry air

/

The imminent engulfed
by memory restructured
communication we summer
in you but for me
its curtains
drawn back this rising
from chairs each setting
their plates and forks
on pools of Elmer's Glue

Vacant signs paint ground breaking narrative for wealth made famous through cathartic bequests of cosmetic rewind. Famine's disavowed blueprints house unspoken moratoriums constructing sightlines from inside ovation's phalangeal divide. By whose landlocked grin should poverty's semi-occupied space forever compound this intermission's anatomically corrected forbearance? Indentured ballerinas are virtually unrecognizable in their heir apparent effort to replicate ocular metonymies spinning astride historical foundations. Mirrored philanthropists fog bifocal lenses figuratively conceding a boundary's conciliatory explanation before the coupling act prescribed.

ACKNOWLEDGEMENTS

Poems from *Iron Lung* have been published by the *Irish Review*, *Cold Mountain Review*, *Poetry Wales*, *Cream City Review*, *Golden Handcuffs Review*, *Lighthouse Journal*, and *OmniVerse*. Thank you to the editors of these journals. To Andre Bagoo and Aaron Kent at Broken Sleep Books, thank you for laying out my unrest. And, to Sangyeon Lee, a thank you instead of a dedication, for *Iron Lung* is not the sort of book you give to someone you love.

LAY OUT YOUR UNREST

www.ingramcontent.com/pod-product-compliance
Lightning Source LLC
Chambersburg PA
CBHW081438090426
42740CB00017B/3348